LA DOLCE VITA
CHAMPAGNE

First published in 1999 by
New Holland Publishers (UK) Ltd
London • Cape Town • Sydney • Auckland

24 Nutford Place
London W1H 6DQ
United Kingdom

80 McKenzie Street
Cape Town 8001
South Africa

Level 1, Unit 4, 14 Aquatic Drive
Frenchs Forest, NSW 2086
Australia

Unit 1A, 218 Lake Road
Northcote
Auckland
New Zealand

10 9 8 7 6 5 4 3 2 1

Copyright © 1999 New Holland Publishers (UK) Ltd

All rights reserved. No part of this publication may be reproduced, stored in a retrieval system, or transmitted in any form or by any means, electronic, mechanical, photocopying, recording or otherwise, without the prior written permission of the publishers and copyright holders.

ISBN 1 85974 159 2

DESIGNED AND EDITED BY
Complete Editions Ltd
40 Castelnau
London SW13 9RU

DESIGNER: Blackjacks
EDITORIAL DIRECTION: Yvonne McFarlane

Reproduction by PICA Colour Separation, Singapore
Printed and bound in Singapore by Tien Wah Press Pte Ltd

Picture Credits: The publishers would like to thank the Champagne Information Bureau, London, for providing much material, Seagram Classics, *Gourmet* magazine, Nicolas Feuillatte Champagne Co., G H Mumm & Co., Pommery Champagne, Pol Roger & Co., Hatch Mansfield Agencies (for Taittinger Champagne), Michael Johnson Ceramics and Riedel Glasses, Fortnum & Mason, Courtauld Institute of Art, Alain Proust/CEPHAS, Nick Rock/CEPHAS, Fred Palmer/CEPHAS, CEPHAS, Grapharchive, the Corcoran Collection, the *New Yorker* and Veuve Clicquot, who sponsor the "English Season". Every effort has been made to identify other illustrations. Any errors or omissions will be corrected in future editions.

CONTENTS

The Story of Champagne..............4
  The Good Dom and the "Jolie Baronne"...6

Grape Expectations 10

Luxuriate! 18
  The Pleasures of Champagne..................18
  Which Glass?...........................23

Beatific Bubbles 24

Getting Fizzical 28

International Imbibing..............46

Food For Thought 54

Up The Avenue 60

Glossary....................................64

THE STORY OF CHAMPAGNE

> *"The night they invented champagne
> It's plain as it can be
> They thought of you and me ..."*
> ALAN JAY LERNER, *GIGI*

An hour's drive east of Paris, the world's most romantic capital, lie the picturesque villages and neatly manicured vineyards of the Champagne region of Northern France that form the home of the world's most romantic wine.

Other wines may have been called "champagnes" and many other sparkling wines may be excellent wines in their own right, but only the officially classified wines from Champagne have the legal right to bear the name of the world's most exclusive wine – a name that evokes glamour, celebration and *joie de vivre*.

Champagne was never actually invented. But Dom Pérignon, monk and cellar-master at the Abbey of Hautvillers 300 years ago, can be regarded as the genius who presided over its development. He refined the process during his 47 years there.

At first, his efforts were directed towards controlling the fizzing in local wines, which was caused by secondary fermentation. In time, the bouquet of bubbles in Dom Pérignon's wines became an attraction rather than an imperfection, bequeathing to us the legacy of champagne we enjoy today. We should be happy to accept the mythology which surrounds him, much of it created long after his death, as we sip what has become the world's most luxurious wine.

THE GOOD DOM AND THE "JOLIE BARONNE"

The early success of champagne was largely due to its popularity at the court of Louis XIV at Versailles, where it made its first appearance via the unlikely route of the confessional at the Abbey of Hautvillers.

Here, local people would confess their sins. Among the good Dom Pérignon's most frequent "visitors" was Jeanne de Thierzy, the "Jolie Baronne" or "pretty baroness", to whom he grudgingly gave continual absolution for her famed infidelities.

In return, she undertook to help promote his wine and offered her exotic favours to the influential, but deeply unattractive, Maréchal de Créqui, if he would deliver a case of it to the court. He did, and Dom Pérignon's champagne was an immediate success, whereupon Louis XIV ordered that a large share of the production be reserved for him.

For her part, the "Jolie Baronne" kept her bargain with the grotesque Maréchal, reportedly saying, "An untroubled eternity is worth one night of love without pleasure".

A carved cask from the Champagne house of Pommery

ATIONS

THE STORY OF CHAMPAGNE

The first champagne houses were formed in Epernay and Reims in the 18th century.

Champagne went out of favour before the French Revolution in 1789, after Louis XVI whimsically declared it unfashionable, leaving only a few old habitués to perk up at the sound of a cork hitting the ceiling. Happily, the fortunes of champagne improved when Napoleon became Emperor of France in 1804.

Emperor Napoleon pays a visit to his old friend, Jean-Rémy Moët, at Epernay

During his time at the military academy at Brienne, the young Napoleon had become a close friend of Jean-Rémy Moët, the son of the founder of the champagne house in Epernay which was to become Moët & Chandon.

While Jean-Rémy became mayor of Epernay, his friend mounted the imperial throne. Since he had a liking for champagne, this was no bad thing for business and before long champagne had regained the rightful status it has held ever since.

There was an explosion of champagne producers, or houses, in the first half of the 19th century. Indeed, many of today's best-known houses were founded in the 25 years after Napoleon's defeat at the Battle of Waterloo in 1815.

The shape of the champagne industry has changed since then, first through erratic family fortunes and then through mergers and takeovers. But what has gone on to consistently greater glory is the fruit of their labours – champagne itself!

GRAPE EXPECT

THE MAKING OF CHAMPAGNE

"I drink champagne when I'm happy, when I'm sad, sometimes when I am alone. I trifle with it when I am not hungry, and I drink it when I am. When I have company I consider it obligatory. Otherwise I never touch it – except when I am thirsty."

MADAME LILY BOLLINGER

Soil unrivalled in the world of vine production, the cool climate, the geography of the area and the carefully selected and tended vines, combine to produce the exceptionally fine grapes from which champagne is created.

Three grape varieties are grown, varieties which complement the chalky soil and micro-climate of the region and blend perfectly to produce wines of consistent quality year on year. They are the black-skinned Pinot Noir, which gives the wine body and long life, the black-skinned Pinot Meunier, which ages quicker, but provides a fruitier bouquet, and the white-skinned Chardonnay, which provides

GRAPE EXPECTATIONS

The first step in making champagne ...

the typical finesse and elegance. By law, these grapes are the only ones allowed in champagne production.

Champagne vineyards must be ploughed three times and fertilized to aerate, clean and enrich the soil. The vines must be pruned in accordance with legally defined rules to limit the quantity of the yield.

Grape-picking begins towards the end of September, one hundred days after the flowering of the vines. The hand-picked and

Examining champagne in the bottle by candle light as it develops in a champagne cellar

GRAPE EXPECTATIONS

sorted grapes are pressed within hours of leaving the vine. The first pressing, the *cuvée*, is followed by two further pressings, the *premières* and *deuxièmes tailles*, or choppings.

The juice flows into open vats or casks for the first fermentation which, in a few weeks, transforms the grape juice into wine. At the end of the winter, when the still wine has become clear after repeated decanting, each cask is evaluated for its specific qualities.

At this point, the blenders' art comes to the fore as they combine the various wines to achieve the characteristic taste of each house, the celebrated *cuvée*. Many of the great houses will also add some of the finest wines from previous years.

After small doses of cane sugar and yeast have been added to the blended still wines, they are bottled, corked and stacked on their sides in the *crayères*, the deep, chalk cellars of Champagne, many of which have been decorated with voluptuous carvings to reflect the sensual nature of the wine as it slowly develops in their chill, dark vaults.

The art of remuage, *which is still performed by hand in the production of the most exclusive champagnes*

The second fermentation, the *méthode champenoise*, takes place inside the bottles, producing the fine mousse of bubbles which is the hallmark of champagne.

Bottles remain in the cellars for an average of three years, during which time a deposit forms inside them. To remove this, the bottles of champagne are placed in sloping racks, or *pupitres*, and systematically turned and tilted, the art of *remuage*, so that the deposit gradually collects on the base of the cork.

Removing the deposit is known as *dégorgement*. The neck of each bottle is plunged head-down into a freezing solution. After the bottle is set upright, the deposit, now a frozen pellet, is forcibly ejected when the cork is removed. The small amount of wine lost during this process is made up by an equal amount of liquor, the *dosage*, a mixture of cane sugar and champagne wine. It is the proportion of sugar used which finally determines the style of champagne. Once the *dégorgement* is completed, the bottle is re-corked with the familiar wire, metal cap and foil, then labelled ready for that tantalizing pop which heralds the first exquisite sip.

The art of dégorgement

LUXUR

THE PLEASURES OF CHAMPAGNE

> "He can make the Statue of Liberty vanish,
> he can make the Capitol vanish for all I care.
> As long as he keeps his hands off my
> uplifting champagne."
> CLAUDIA SCHIFFER,
> ON ILLUSIONIST FIANCÉ, DAVID COPPERFIELD

Miracle of the earth, perfected by the winemaker's genius, champagne is, *par excellence*, the wine for all moods and occasions. It is a wine to wake with, a wine to recover with, a wine to pass the day with and a wine to herald unforgettable nights.

As befits such a perfect companion, champagne comes in bottles to suit all occasions. These range from the 18.75 cl (sometimes 20 cl) quarter bottle for a quick solo refresher, through the 37.5 cl half-bottle for an intimate, shared experience, to the 75 cl full bottle, enough for six good glasses, ideal as an aperitif for four. The two-bottle magnum

19 CHAMPAGNE

supplies the optimum amount for an all-champagne dinner party for four. For sheer extravagance, work your way through the four-bottle Jeroboam to the eccentricity of the Salmanazar (12 bottles) and the Nebuchadnezzar (20 bottles).

Champagne should be drunk chilled, but not ice-cold. A couple of hours in the door of a refrigerator, or thirty minutes in an ice bucket, should suffice.

Access to this seductive drink is easier than it sometimes appears. Hold the bottle in one hand towards the base, pointing the neck away from yourself, and anyone else, and undo the foil and wire around the cork. Tilt the bottle slightly and rotate it, while holding firmly onto the cork; turning the bottle and not the cork gives greater leverage. The bottle "should open smoothly with a gentle sigh, like a contented woman", as the roués of old would

KEEPING YOUR COOL

The ultimate champagne wrap to keep your fizz cool has been created by Givenchy's outrageous fashion designer, Alexander McQueen, for the house of Pommery.

This is of electric blue snakeskin and enhances a bottle of Pommery Brut Royale. At around £60 (US$90), it is a snip at Bloomingdales, in New York, Harrods, in London, and other top international stores.

LUXURIATE!

have us believe. There should be no spurt of wine. Make of that what you will.

Pour a little champagne into each glass to let it fizz up and quickly settle before you gradually fill them. This avoids the wine frothing uncontrollably over the top of the glass, which happens if you try to pour too much too quickly.

WHICH GLASS?

In England, the Victorians, along with their contemporaries in the rest of the world, favoured the saucer-shaped glass, the "coupe". Would they have used it if they had known that it was rumoured to have been modelled on the Empress Josephine's (some say Mme de Pompadour's) breasts? In the coupe, however, champagne's fine mousse is dissipated too quickly and its bouquet squandered.

The "flute" is favoured today, a tall elegant glass with straight sides.

Serious imbibers prefer the "tulip". This has gently curved sides, the mouth being narrower than the bowl. Connoisseurs will tell you that a glass this shape enhances the bouquet in champagne while encouraging the mousse to rise in a long-lasting, sparkling stream.

BEATIFIC BUBBLES

*"Here's to champagne, the drink divine
That makes us forget our troubles.
It's made of a dollar's worth of wine
And three dollar's worth of bubbles."*
ANON

Over the centuries, the style and taste of champagne has changed dramatically.

Originally, it was a sweet wine, as the founding fathers could not control the fermentation with today's finesse and depended heavily on the introduction of sugar into the wine.

The driest is Brut, followed in ascending order of sweetness by Sec and Demi-Sec, both of which suggest dryness, but are, in fact, sweet. The amount of sugar added, expressed as a percentage, would roughly mean one per cent for a dry wine, rising to four per cent for a sweet wine.

The courtiers of Alexander II, Tsar of Russia from 1855 to 1881, who gulped champagne out of their favourite ballerina's slippers, demanded champagne with a sweetness of 12 per cent, a syrupy confection specially made for the Russian market.

BEATIFIC BUBBLES

Vintage champagne, *millésime*, is wine made only from the grapes of one year when the vintage has been particularly fine. Each champagne house has its own style, which is invariably fuller than non-vintage versions.

Unlike the wines of Bordeaux or Burgundy, "vintage", where champagne is concerned, does not mean better. It means different. And not everyone likes these heavier flavours; you should never fear expressing a preference for good non-vintage champagne.

There are three basic styles of champagne: those made with the traditional mix of the three champagne grapes; those made with white grapes only, Blancs de Blancs; and those made with Blancs de Noirs, a white wine made from black grapes.

Pink champagne used to be considered an oddity and until recent years was a rarity. Before the 1970s, it was hard to find in high street wine shops. But then Prince Charles gave it a boost in Britain, when he served a Bollinger rosé the night before his wedding to Lady Diana Spencer and there followed a pink explosion.

Rosé champagne is correctly made by allowing the skins of the black Pinot grapes to tint the wine, but more commonly by adding a small amount of the Champenois, still red wine from Bouzy, as part of the *dosage*. Its heart-warming hue adds extra sparkle and romance to any champagne occasion.

FIZZ

28 LA DOLCE VITA

If becoming intimate with someone is your expressed purpose, what better way to achieve it than by sharing a bottle of champagne, either as an exquisite prelude or a delicious coda?

The question is which champagne to choose? Here are some suggestions.

BOLLINGER

The Bollinger style is big and beefy, bringing out the full flavour through traditional methods of ageing and the use of their special reserved wines in blending. Even the non-vintage Special Cuvée contains a high proportion of these reserves. Bollinger produce a rare superb Blancs de Noirs, their Vieilles Vignes Françaises. It is the ultimate in flowery, flattering excellence. If the occasion (and your companion) demands something extra special, but your budget doesn't run to one of the highest priced champagnes, this is the one for you.

> *"Champagne is like music. It has to be identified by name. You don't say 'I've listened to music'; you say 'I've listened to Mozart or Berlioz.' It's the same with champagne. You need to know who is behind the label."*
> REMI KRUG

GETTING
ICAL

CHARLES HEIDSIECK

Of the three houses bearing the name Heidsieck, this is the one to go for when you want to make your intentions unmistakable. The founder, Charles-Emile Heidsieck was the original Champagne Charlie, a name that followed his successful forays into the American market in the middle of the 19th century.

A colourful character, he became embroiled in the American Civil War while on an undercover mission (disguised as a piano player on a Mississippi paddle steamer) to recover debts in New Orleans. The Charles Heidsieck prestige cuvée is, not surprisingly, called Champagne Charlie. To set things off with a rakish, devil-may-care flair, you can't go wrong with this.

KRUG

This Emperor of champagnes, this sun in the firmament of champagne is everything champagne should be. Krug have always purveyed fine, expensive wines, full-bodied and serious, with a nutty nose. This is the only house which makes exclusively prestige wines. Krug's wines are "hand-made – blended with our hearts, not just science" says proprietor Rémi Krug.

Often as many as 50 different wines from 25 villages go into their Grande Cuvée. Vintages to kill for include those from Clos du Mesnil, made from the vines of that small vineyard at Mesnil-sur-Oger which looks exactly as it did in 1698.

Californian wine guru, Robert Mondavi, summed up the appreciation of Krug fans the world over when he commented, "It has a beautiful after-taste. I don't like champagnes that are too acid. Krug is beautifully harmonious and delicate."

When beauty, harmony and delicacy are your immediate concerns, go for Krug every time and hang the price.

LANSON

This house was founded in Reims in 1760 by François Delamotte; the Lansons were partners who took control in the 1850s. They grow almost three-quarters of their own grapes on large estates bought in the 1930s by brothers Henri and Victor Lanson (the latter, by all accounts, loved his own product a little too much). The blend of their Lanson Black Label has never been accurately revealed, possibly because it changes so often. The house style is light and lively, even slightly acidic. Their luxury label is the Noble Cuvée, but their mass-produced, yet high quality wines are always a good buy.

GETTING FIZZICAL

The 1915 Lanson sealed the life-long romance between the Duke and Duchess of Windsor and the internationally renowned author Frederic Raphael looks to Lanson Black Label for inspiration. Among regularly consumed marques, this has style and panache.

MILLENNIUM MARQUES

The millennium celebrations are going to provide golden moments for champagne drinkers and champagne producers.

Roederer have produced 2,000 Methuselahs (each containing the equivalent of eight full bottles) of the 1990 vintage at a staggering £1,350 (US$2,000) each – but only a few remain.

Veuve Clicquot unveiled the Trillennium Cuvée of 1989 and sold out immediately. Seek one out from a specialist wine merchant. The champagne house of Salon plan to release magnums of its 1983 at up to £150 (US$225) each.

Moët & Chandon, together with Pol Roger and Taittinger, are still keeping their plans dark, but they will be producing special cuvées for the event.

As usual, confident Krug feel no need to produce anything special, as all Krug is special. One regular customer has already reserved £500,000 (US$800,000) worth of their splendid bubbly to mark this unique occasion.

LAURENT-PERRIER

Originally founded in 1823 at Tours-sur-Marne, east of Epernay, by Eugène Laurent, Laurent-Perrier produce wines that are generally flowery, light and delicate. Laurent-Perrier also make a traditional rosé which has been a long-standing favourite fizz at society parties on both sides of the Atlantic. The company also makes a bone-dry Ultra Brut, another "statement" champagne which shows you mean business.

Laurent-Perrier's grandest wine is the Grand Siècle, which many regard as equal to Dom Pérignon or Roederer Cristal. Go for this to show an individual streak and sense of style.

MOËT & CHANDON

Ever since the firm was founded by Claude Moët in 1743 it has remained a main force in the world of champagne. With its subsidiaries, Mercier and Ruinart, it now produces a quarter of total champagne sales.

Madame de Pompadour was a devoted customer and Napoleon Bonaparte was a friend of Claude's son Jean-Rémy while he was at the military school at Brienne. In 1832, Jean-Rémy's

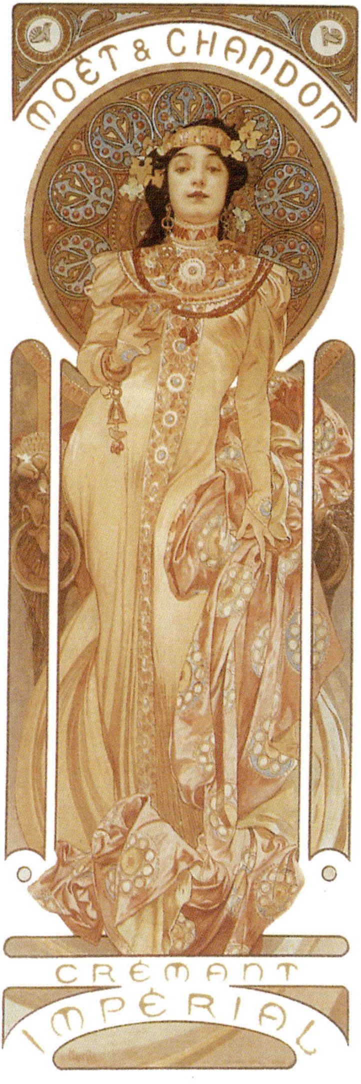
MOËT & CHANDON
CRÉMANT
IMPÉRIAL

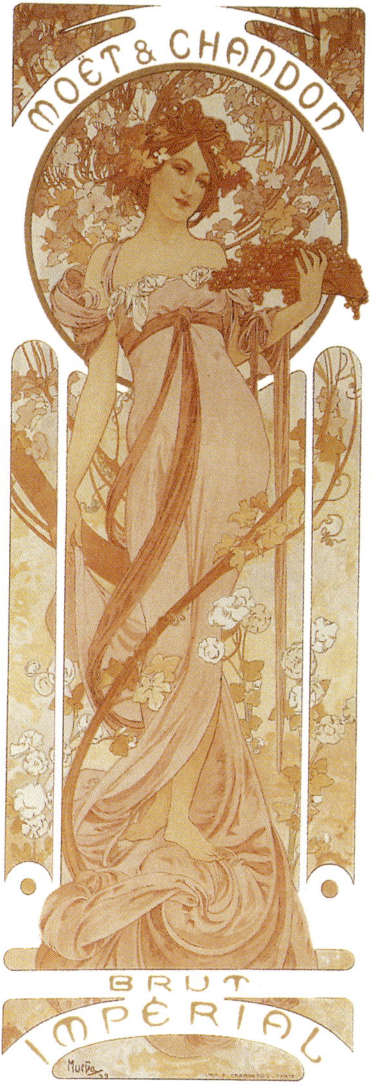
MOËT & CHANDON
BRUT
IMPÉRIAL

son-in-law, the Comte Chandon de Briailles, added his name to the company's title.

The best-selling wine made by Moët & Chandon, Brut Imperial, is of consistently good quality, with a rich, gold colour.

The luxury wine to aspire for is Moët & Chandon's Dom Pérignon, with its distinctive bottle shape and dark green label. With an impeccable flavour and bouquet, it has been a marketing triumph, boosted by the fact that the house owns the Abbey of Hautvillers, where the legendary Dom Pérignon evolved the champagne process.

Film star Joan Collins can often be seen in the Moët hospitality marquee at polo or racing, but she also has a taste for Dom Pérignon when she is letting her hair down at a Tramp nightclub.

With a pedigree of seduction that stretches back to the earliest days of champagne and the Jolie Baronne, there's no mistaking the allure and promise that a bottle of Dom Pérignon brings.

G. H. MUMM

This champagne house was founded in 1827 by two German immigrants in Reims, Peter-Arnold Mumm and Frederick Giesler. It was Mumm's son, Georg-Hermann, who developed the eye-catching Cordon Rouge label.

Highly sales-orientated and with an eye to clever marketing, they produced provocative posters at the turn of the 20th century – a tradition that lives on. They did not bother to acquire French citizenship and the company was confiscated in the First World War. Some think Cordon Rouge is an unadventurous drink, but the label looks good, and many prefer it to more prestigious and expensive marques. If Mumm happens to be your favoured fizz, serve it without hesitation – your pleasure and satisfaction will only add to its seductive charms.

G.H.MUMM & Cº
LA PLUS HAUTE QUALITÉ
CARACTÉRISE LES
CHAMPAGNES G.H.MUMM & Cº

Champagne Pommery.
Dieu que la vie de tous les jours est jolie !

PERRIER-JOUËT

This Epernay house was founded by Pierre-Nicolas-Marie Perrier in 1811. He added his wife's maiden name to avoid confusion with Joseph Perrier's house at Châlons. This is one of the most supremely elegant of the non-vintage champagnes, with a truly distinctive style.

Perrier-Jouët's prestige wine arrives in a prestige bottle designed by Emile Gallé. It bears enamelled anemones in Art Nouveau style which swirl around the bottle. And inside, the bubbly lives up to its elegant, if somewhat raffish, surroundings.

This is a champagne to serve with a twinkle in the eye, one that conjures up the timeless charms of the Parisian Belle Epoque.

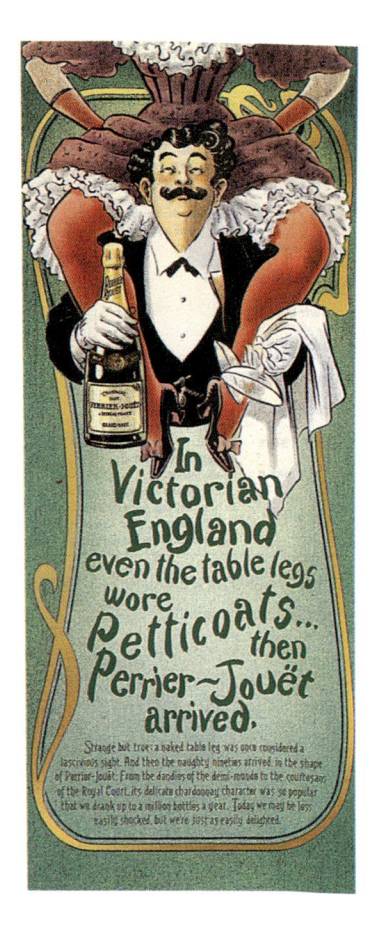

POL ROGER

Founded in 1849 by M. Pol Roger, it was his son, Maurice, who brought the house to greatness during the First World War and it is still run by the same family. Pol Roger's prestige wine, Cuvée Sir Winston Churchill, is less beefy than some vintages.

Pol Roger was a particular favourite of Maria Callas and the great diva often took a glass or two to soothe her vocal chords.

The company produces some outstanding rosé, of a deep pink hue, heavily weighted to the Pinot Noir grape. This is elegant and delicious and caresses the palate with a stream of tiny bubbles.

TWO PRINCES AND THE DUKE

Champagne has long been a favourite with royalty, particularly British royalty. Princes Charles and Andrew both favoured Bollinger for their wedding receptions.

Champagne was always a favourite on the jazz scene, particularly in New Orleans, where it was so common it was referred to simply as "wine". Perrier-Jouët used the occasion of Duke Ellington's 70th birthday to launch their prestige Belle Epoque. Paul Krug celebrated his honeymoon by following the great jazz-man on tour.

LOUIS ROEDERER

Louis Roederer and Krug are widely regarded as the two finest makers of champagne.

Louis Roederer came from Strasbourg in 1827 to work with his uncle. He inherited the firm six years later and transformed it, largely by expanding the Russian market. He created the hallmark clear bottle at the request of Tsar Nicholas I of Russia.

The house produces an unusually high percentage of its own grapes (some 80 per cent, which gives their tipple remarkable consistency) and has produced a record-breaking number of vintage wines. It holds considerable reserves of wine which have aged in both wood and bottle. In total, Louis Roederer produces only some 220,000 cases a year, which explains both the price and the consistency. There are myriad vintage styles, the pinnacle being the glorious Cristal which is perfection.

Raymond Blanc, the French chef-owner of the acclaimed Le Manoir aux Quat' Saisons in Oxfordshire, England, heads a distinguished list of connoisseurs for whom this is their number one champagne. Among them is Hollywood novelist, Jackie Collins, who is devoted to Cristal, perhaps because it is the house champagne of Tramp, the celebrated nightclubs in Los Angeles and London owned by her husband.

Quite simply the best – you can't fail with Roederer Cristal.

L'INSTANT
TAITTINGER
TAITTINGER
CHAMPAGNE
TAITTINGER
TAITTINGER
BRUT
CHAMPAGNE
TAITTINGER
BRUT

TAITTINGER

Pierre Taittinger was based at the great Château Marquetterie, south of Epernay, during the First World War. In 1930, he returned to buy it and its associated vineyards. He also bought two cellars, one under the 13th-century abbey of St Nicaise. Elegance is the keyword for Taittinger with the lightness and perfume of Chardonnay grapes coming through. This is fitting as Count Thibaut IV of Champagne brought back the first Chardonnay grapes from Palestine in the 13th century and it is in his banqueting hall that this house entertains. Tattinger's prestige wine is the Comtes de Champagne, a Blancs de Blancs of true magnificence, which also is available as a rosé.

The Cuvée de Prestige is a particular favourite of Inès de la Fressange, the Chanel model, who has inspired many of Karl Lagerfeld's designs.

VEUVE CLICQUOT-PONSARDIN

Founded in 1772 by a merchant in Reims, the company was brought to prominence by his formidable widow, Nicole-Barbe Clicquot-Ponsardin (La Veuve Clicquot or Widow Clicquot) after she inherited the business in 1805. A champagne legend in her own lifetime, she created the orange label which adorns their non-vintage Brut.

The Widow, the yellow-label Brut, is still the company's major seller, accounting for over 80 per cent of the production. The house's luxury vintage is the rich and chocolatey La Grande Dame.

Superstar authoress Jilly Cooper fell in love with Clicquot when following the royal polo set to chukkas worldwide, while researching her novel *Polo*. Coincidentally, Clicquot are major sponsors of the game.

INTERN
IMBI

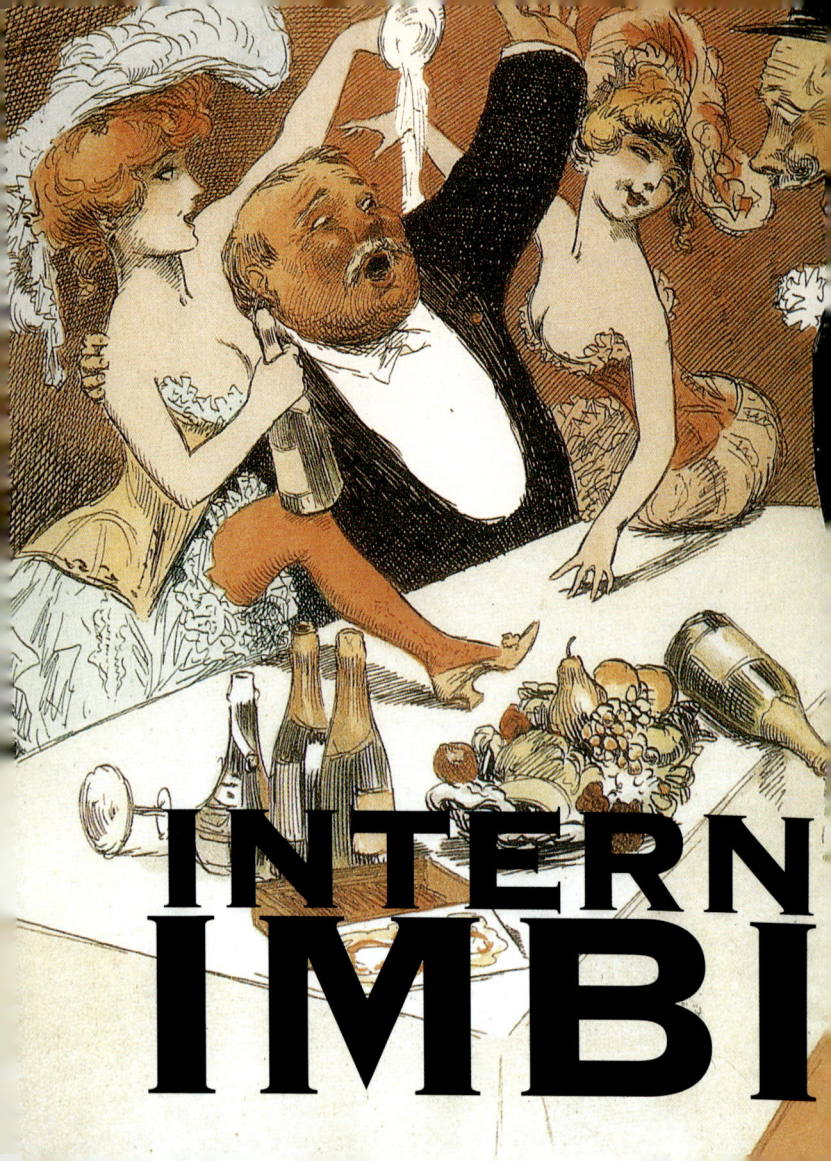

> *"For two intimates, lovers or comrades, to spend a quiet evening with a magnum, drinking no aperitif before, nothing but a glass or two of cognac after – that is the ideal."*
> EVELYN WAUGH

To savour the delights of champagne to the full, treat yourself to some of those memory milestones that linger in the mind for ever.

Whether you opt for a glass of chilled champagne while you sample an ounce of Sevruga or Osietra caviar at Caviar Kaspia in the Place de la Madeleine, or cool yourself with a glass beneath the Mediterranean sun as you eye up the international film set on the terrace of the Hôtel Martinez in Cannes.

Whether you summon up a bottle of Bolly to pass the evening in Annabel's or mingle with New York's finest in the Polo Lounge and Restaurant in the Westbury Hotel on Madison Avenue – all of the world's great cities offer somewhere unique for those special champagne moments.

Best of all, try champagne in Champagne. Reims and Epernay, and the small surrounding villages will spoil you for choice, but if sampling the best the region has to offer in one of its great

ATIONAL
BING

châteaux appeals, treat yourself to a stay at Boyer-les-Crayères. Now one of France's most luxurious hotels, this was once the magnificent home of the Pommery family (of champagne fortune). Standing in parkland outside Reims, the hotel has a superb restaurant that provides the ideal setting in which to enjoy a memorable meal accompanied by a choice bottle of bubbly.

As you would expect, there are equally rich pickings in Paris. But for a quick fix of Parisian social life at its best, try the Brasserie Lipp, on the Blvd St Germain. The rendezvous for *le tout*

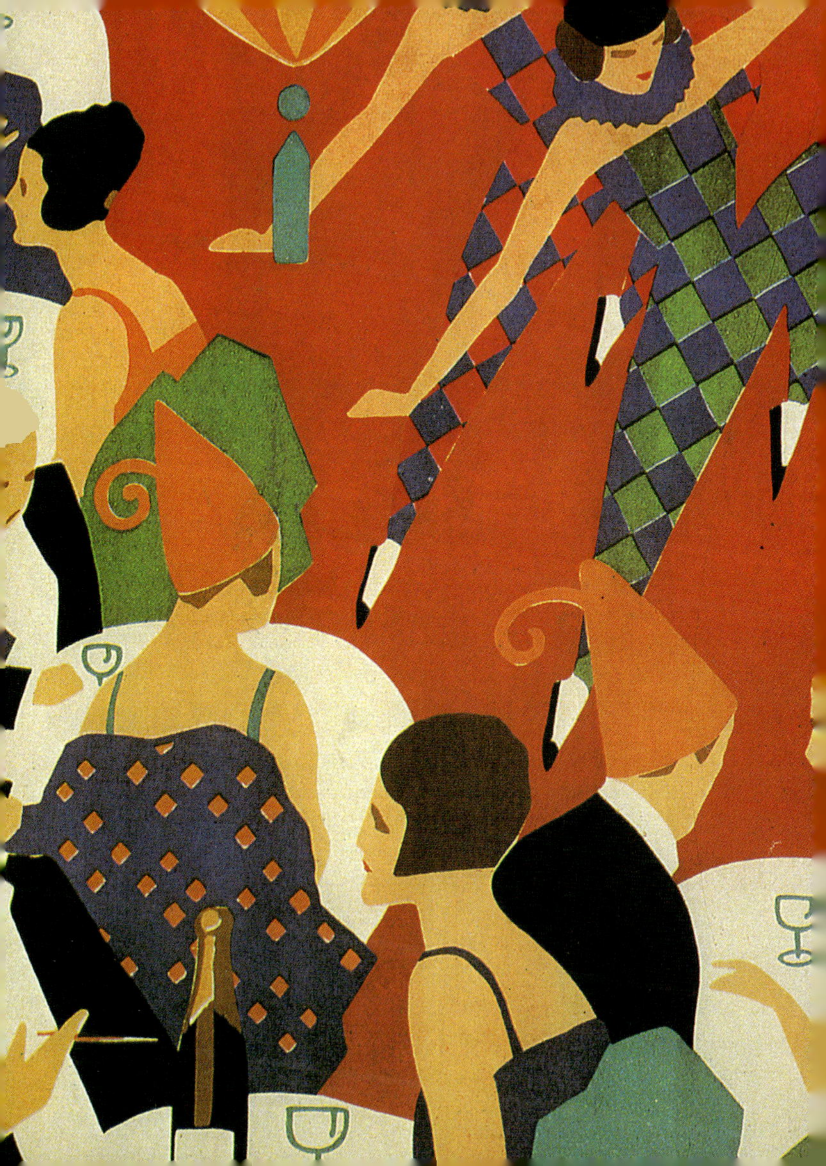

INTERNATIONAL IMBIBING

Errol Flynn and friends bringing the glamour of champagne to Hollywood

Paris, this quintessential Parisian café is the haunt of the glamorous and fashionable through the night. Arrive late (everyone does) and order a bottle of champagne to while away the small hours until dawn.

Heading south, try a smart glass at the Eden Roc on Cap d'Antibes, or a friendly glass opposite the Red Pear Theatre in Vielles Antibes.

Monte Carlo can offer splendours, but at a price if you choose the Hôtel de Paris. On the other hand, the "in" crowd, including a sprinkling of European royals, can be found at the Stars and Bars on the old port.

Harry's Bar, Calle Vallaresso, in Venice, is the most famous bar in this celebrated city. Harry's Bar is also the home of the Bellini, the cocktail made from fresh peach juice and champagne. Always busy, always fun, here the ghosts of Hemingway and Orson Welles and faded European royalty rub shoulders with the smartest of Europe's smart set.

INTERNATIONAL IMBIBING

In London, you can enjoy a huge range of bounteous bubbly at Kettners, one of the city's first specialist champagne bars. Favoured by media and theatre people, it promotes its own champagne at very good prices, alongside virtually every other great name, in bottles of various sizes.

Discerning visitors to Sydney order half-a-dozen freshwater oysters at the Rockpool, to slip down with a good bottle of bubbly. They won't be offended that you haven't ordered one of the excellent Oz fizzes.

When in Perth, inveigle your way into the Yacht Club, to sip and sip as the colourful sails billow past. This is serious yachting and quaffing territory.

INTERNATIONAL IMBIBING

PERFECT GROOMING

Guests invited to the 1949 wedding of the fabulously wealthy Aly Khan and the Hollywood superstar, Rita Hayworth, enjoyed a reception few were ever likely to forget. Fifteen bottles of champagne were earmarked for each guest!

But that was only a prelude to the groom's generosity. His bride was given a massive cash dowry, a string of racehorses, and an Alfa-Romeo, along with miscellaneous diamonds and rubies.

In New York . . . well, in New York just drink champagne. A great deal of life there is dedicated to it, at the Carlyle Hotel on East 76th Street, while listening to Bobby Short, at the Algonquin on West 44th Street, while listening to Steve Ross. The only downside is that both will probably sing:

> *"I get no kick from champagne,*
> *Mere alcohol doesn't thrill me at all . . .*
> *But I get a kick out of you."*

Alternatively, you might try the Top of the Tower, Beekman Tower, at Mitchell Plaza. This may not be the highest hotel-top lounge in New York but, halfway to heaven, it is among the most elegant and appropriate settings in Manhattan to celebrate the triumphs of champagne in the world's most vibrant city.

INTERNATIONAL IMBIBING

Cross to LA and settle yourself into the Polo Lounge at the Beverley Hills Hotel. Still pretty and still pulling international celebrities, the Polo Lounge has been the social epicentre of Hollywood since its heyday. Allow time to savour the atmosphere (and see who happens to drop by) by ordering a full bottle and relishing every sip.

Champagne is an important detail in Manet's Bar at the Folies Bergère

FO
FOR

OD
THOUGHT

*"And we meet, with champagne
and a chicken, at last."*
LADY MARY WORTLEY MONTAGU,
18TH-CENTURY ENGLISH WRITER

Champagne and chicken, champagne and strawberries, champagne and oysters, champagne and caviar – simple classic combinations which evoke summer days, balmy nights, romantic trysts and louche liaisons. Can there be any more suggestive supper than slurping oysters and sipping champagne?

But there is much more to enjoying champagne at the table for, rarely among the world's wines, champagne can be sipped and savoured right through a meal. Still wine may be the automatic choice, but bubbly, especially a vintage when you can afford it, will enhance most dishes from simple starters, through rich cream-based main courses, to chocolate (yes, chocolate!) desserts and cheese.

A champagne breakfast is the perfect way to start the day. Try champagne with scrambled eggs and smoked salmon at the Ritz in Paris (they'll even bring it to your room at two in the morning), with a simple *pain au chocolat* or a selection of exotic fruits.

For the main meals of the day, fruity vintages enhance plain grilled fish, while a Blanc de Blancs will cut through a rich hollandaise or other buttery sauce. Substantial beef dishes really need to be matched with beefy vintages, but these, such as Taittinger Comtes de Champagne, can make heavy demands on the bank balance.

In the region of Champagne itself, vintage champagne is recommended to accompany the local Brie.

Oriental spices present the biggest test, and again it is the great vintages which rise to the occasion and offer the greatest satisfaction. However, it has been reported that both Laurent-Perrier and Pol Roger non-vintages have coped well with mild curry and saffron-based sauces. Thai food and other dishes with sweet-and-sour sauces provide even greater challenges, but one noted restaurateur took the problem head-on and served a demi-sec champagne, with great success.

And so to chocolate, the gourmet's delight. Chocolate coats the palate and restricts access to the tastebuds for the champagne. But with dark chocolate concoctions, once

St Matthew Passion
Johann Sebastian Bach

FOOD FOR THOUGHT

again demi-sec comes to the rescue to complete the ultimate gastronomic treat.

For many, champagne is the wine for picnics. These should at best consist of quail's eggs, followed by simple fishy finger food: prawns, smoked salmon, skewered scallops and chunks of lobster. If these are dressed with a freshly made mayonnaise, aim for a lemony-fresh champagne. Follow with pink lamb cutlets and a rosé. Nothing in cloying pastry really works, except a slice of a good game pie, accompanied by a nutty or fruity vintage.

The main problem is transporting suitably chilled bubbly to the picnic. It deserves a seat of its own, not to be packed into the back of the car and shaken around. Allow this noble drink time to settle before opening. And then enjoy!

THE ULTIMATE ACCESSORY

Glasses are such a bore at picnics, so why not avail yourself of the essential accessory – a champagne straw?

A creation of Asprey & Garrard, it is available from their emporia in London and New York, as well as at the Beverley Hills Hotel in Los Angeles.

Drop hints and have one at birthday time. After all, it's only £60 (US$90).

UP THE AVENUE

VISITING CHAMPAGNE

> *"In his blue gardens, men and girls came and went like moths among the whisperings and the champagne and the stars."*
>
> F. Scott Fitzgerald, *The Great Gatsby*

If you are a champagne lover intent on savouring the delights of the region, there are circular, signposted tours to follow by car. Along these Routes de Champagne many grower-producers offer guided tours. Some have atmospheric accommodation, perfect for a champagne tryst, complete with candlelit dinner.

CHAMPAGNE
CHAMPAGNE
CHAMPAGNE
CHAMPAGNE
CHAMPAGNE
BRUT
GRANDE RESERVE
CHAMPAGNE
Brut
BRUT
MAISON

UP THE AVENUE

Hard at work on the vines of Champagne

But for a first, awe-inspiring visit nothing can compare with a long stroll or car ride in Reims or Epernay. The great names are prominently, but tastefully, displayed, and their sumptuous mansions can be glimpsed behind imposing wrought iron gates. Most organize visits and tastings. These are sometimes free, but mostly there is a small charge for tasting, with supplements for the weightier vintages. After all, who would expect free glasses of Dom Ruinart, Dom Pérignon or La Grande Dame?

In Reims, **RUINART** (03-26 77 51 54) has tours by appointment only, with a free tasting of their non-vintage. There is a charge to taste all five in their range. **POMMERY** (03-26 61 62 59) have free multilingual tours every half-an-hour. **VEUVE CLICQUOT PONSARDIN** (03-26 89 54 41) offers free tours which include a tasting of their Brut Yellow

UP THE AVENUE

Label. Anything more exotic is charged for. **TAITTINGER** (03-26 85 45 35) charge for their tour and tasting, which is hardly surprising. The latter three houses do not need appointments, but do check times and advise in advance if you need an English-speaking guide. **MUMM** (03-26 49 59 69) and **PIPER-HEIDSIECK** (03-26 84 43 44) also offer tours.

In Epernay, **MERCIER** (03-26 54 75 26) charge to visit their exotically carved *crayères* and sell everything from jeroboams to sweatshirts. **MOËT & CHANDON** (03-26 54 71 11) have a range of tours and **PERRIER-JOUËT** (03-26 55 20 53) welcome visitors by appointment only.

In the outlying villages, notable houses well worth a detour include **AYALA** (03-26 55 15 44) and **BOLLINGER** (03-26 53 33 66) in Ay, who entertain visitors by appointment only, as do **LAURENT-PERRIER** (03-26 58 77 29) at Tours-sur-Marne. At Chouilly, seek out the newish house of **NICOLAS FEUILLATTE** (03-26 59 55 60) which produces a consistently good quaffing champagne.

A timeless view of Champagne vineyards recalling the days of Dom Pérignon

Detailed information of charges and times is readily available in the Champagne area from the tourist offices in Reims and Epernay. But one thing is sure, for this is France, they are all closed for lunch.

GLOSSARY

BLANCS DE BLANCS White wine from white grapes only.

BLANCS DE NOIRS White wine from black grapes only.

BRUT Dry champagne, with only 15 g (0.5 oz) of sugar per litre (1.75 pt).

CREMANT Champagne with half the normal sparkle.

LE CRU The growth of a quality grape, from one vineyard.

UNE CUVE A vat.

LA CUVEE The blend.

LA DOSAGE The topping-up mixture of sugar and wine used in the making of champagne.

DOUX Sweet champagne with over 50 g (1.76 oz) of sugar per litre (1.75pt).

GRAND CRU fine growth, top quality vineyard.

LA MARQUE The brand.

MILLESIME Vintage year.

LA MOUSSE The bubbles in champagne.

NEGOCIANT A shipper of champagne.

PUPITRE The slotted rack on which champagne bottles are riddled.

REMUAGE Riddling bottles of champagne to remove deposits.

SEC Medium dry champagne with 17–23 g (0.6–0.8 oz) of sugar per litre (1.75 pt).

LES TAILLES Grape juice produced after the first pressing.

VIN DE CUVEE The first pressing of 2,000 l (440 gal) of champagne.